DIANE SEED'S
PASTA
cooking

D1325408

First published in Great Britain in 2002 by Ebury Press
for WHSmith, Greenbridge Road, Swindon SN3 3LD

1 3 5 7 9 10 8 6 4 2

Text © Diane Seed 2002
Photographs © Ebury Press 2002

Ebury Press
Random House, 20 Vauxhall Bridge Road, London SW1V 2SA

Random House Australia (Pty) Limited
20 Alfred Street, Milsons Point, Sydney, New South Wales 2061, Australia

Random House New Zealand Limited
18 Poland Road, Glenfield, Auckland 10, New Zealand

Random House South Africa (Pty) Limited
Endulini, 5A Jubilee Road, Parktown 2193, South Africa

The Random House Group Limited Reg. No. 954009

www.randomhouse.co.uk

A CIP catalogue record for this book is available from the British Library.

Editor: Gillian Haslam
Designer: Christine Wood
Photographer: Craig Robertson
Food Stylist: Jules Beresford
Stylist: Helen Trent

ISBN 0091884101

Papers used by Ebury Press are natural, recyclable products made from wood grown in
sustainable forests.

Printed and bound in Italy by Graphicom Srl

CONTENTS

Title page: Tagliatelle with Mushroom Sauce, page 28

Above: Fettuccine with Chicken Livers, page 84

INTRODUCTION

In Italy, every region is justly proud of its culinary heritage and fine local produce, and traditional dishes are still prepared with love and skill. Often, a recipe varies from town to town, or family to family, but the common source remains obvious. Today, there is also a 'new' style of cooking, often pioneered by local restaurants who have rediscovered old, forgotten recipes, or adapted firm favourites to make them lighter and more suited to the modern way of life.

These new recipes use regional produce in fresh, exciting ways and have given an extra zest and vitality to Italian cooking. The ones I have happily included in this selection of recipes were created with care and a deep respect for local ingredients. Most of the recipes serve four people as a main course, but you could also serve them as a starter in which case they will feed six.

COOKING PASTA

Tagliatelle with Shellfish and Sweet Peppers,
page 53

Good quality dry pasta is hard to beat, so there is really no need to make fresh pasta at home unless you want to experiment with unusual dough mixtures and interesting fillings.

Dry pasta should be cooked in a large, tall saucepan, using at least 4 litres (7 pints) of water and 2 tablespoons of salt for 500 g (1 lb) of pasta. The water must be brought to a brisk boil and the salt dissolved before the pasta is added. Long pasta must be eased in gently and the pan should be partially covered to bring the water back to the boil as

quickly as possible. The pasta should be stirred frequently (ideally with a wooden fork) to keep the strands separate.

You need to watch the pasta carefully so that it is not overcooked – no Italian would ever leave the kitchen while cooking pasta! Ignore any preconceived ideas about cooking time, and from time to time lift out and sample a small piece of pasta. The pasta is cooked when it is still firm in the centre and offers some resistance to the bite. In Italian this is known as *al dente*.

Today there are splendid tall pasta pans with built-in colanders that enable you to drain the pasta quickly with much less risk of scalding your hands and over-draining the pasta. The pasta should always be slightly shiny from the drops of water trapped between the coils, and a little pasta cooking water is often added to the sauce if it seems slightly dry.

In traditional trattorias you often see the cook tossing the freshly drained pasta into a large, heavy frying pan containing the sauce, his arm muscles rippling as he rotates the heavy pan to incorporate all of the pasta into his sauce. Most of us don't have a large enough frying pan, or enough muscle to emulate this very effective way of combining sauce and pasta, but I have discovered that a light, non-stick wok provides the perfect alternative. I make many sauces in my wok and the wider diameter makes it very easy to stir in the pasta, which can be served piping hot straight from the wok.

Although most recipes specify a certain type of pasta, you can of course use whatever shape you have to hand.

Pasta with Anchovies, page 57

CHOOSING THE INGREDIENTS

In order to make successful pasta dishes, good olive oil should be used and the Parmesan cheese should be bought in a piece and freshly grated for each recipe. It will keep for some time wrapped in foil and stored in the refrigerator.

With all the recipes here, if you cannot find specific ingredients, you should feel free to improvise and adapt the recipe. When anchovies are required, you can use the whole anchovies preserved in salt or the fillets in oil. Chillies vary in strength from plant to plant. It is often better to dry some chillies and grind them up so that you begin to know the fire in your particular mixture.

Some recipes use fresh tomatoes in the sauce. Although these will give the best taste, you can replace them with the same quantity of drained, tinned tomatoes if you wish. To peel fresh tomatoes, plunge them briefly into a bowl of boiling water, remove with a slotted spoon and the skin will be easy to remove.

MAKING FRESH PASTA

This is the basic recipe for making delicate golden sheets of pasta.

Use one egg to every 100 g (3½ oz) of strong plain flour. Arrange the flour in a mound on the table with a well in the centre. Break the eggs into this well and use a fork to draw the flour gradually into the eggs. A pinch of salt is sometimes added at this stage. Once all the egg has

into the flour, knead the dough energetically on a clean, floured surface using the heel of your hand for ten minutes. If the mixture is too sticky, a little more flour may be added. (It is not possible to be too precise because eggs vary in size and even flour varies from country to country.) If you are making large quantities it is easier to divide the dough into two or three balls and work separately, keeping the remaining balls covered with plastic film or kitchen foil. Some people prefer to use a food processor to make life easier.

Roll the pasta out on a lightly floured large wooden board so that some moisture is absorbed, using a rolling pin about 80 cm (30 in) long. Alternatively, a hand-cranked pasta machine makes it very easy to produce uniformly fine sheets. Allow the pasta sheet to dry for about 30 minutes, then fold it into a loose, flat roll about 5 cm (2 in) wide and cut into the desired widths. These are then shaken out, arranged in little piles, and allowed to dry for at least 15 minutes.

If you want to make stuffed pasta, the dough is made in the same way using two eggs and one egg yolk to 240 g (8 oz) flour and a pinch of salt. With stuffed pasta, the pasta sheet must not be allowed to dry. Use either a fluted pastry wheel or pastry cutter to cut out the desired shape, working as quickly as possible. The cooking time will depend on the weight of the filling and the thickness of the pasta used so there is no hard and fast rule. You will have to keep testing.

Fresh Pasta with Herbs, Tomato and Cheese, page 14

TOMATO SAUCE

2 tbsp olive oil

1 medium onion, peeled and finely
   chopped

2 cloves garlic, peeled and finely
   chopped

2 x 400 g (12 oz) cans Italian plum
   tomatoes

salt and black pepper

Many recipes call for a basic tomato sauce. There are countless regional variations, but this recipe is a fairly universal one.

Heat the oil and gently fry the onion and garlic until soft. Add the tomatoes, with their juice, squashing them with the back of a wooden spoon. Cook uncovered over a high heat until the sauce thickens. Season to taste and then blend to a thick mixture in a food processor or blender.

Rigatoni Stuffed with Fish, page 70

PASTA
with vegetables

TAGLIATELLE WITH RICOTTA CHEESE AND FRESH HERBS

SERVES: 4   PREPARATION: 5 MINS   COOKING: 10 MINS

INGREDIENTS

60 g (2 oz) fresh herbs such as
    basil, tarragon, parsley and dill
30 g (1 oz) shelled walnuts
500 g (1 lb) tagliatelle
salt and black pepper
3⅓ tbsp olive oil
250 g (8 oz) ricotta cheese
60 g (2 oz) freshly grated Parmesan
    cheese

NUTRITION

Each portion contains:

Energy: 730 calories

Fat: 28 g of which saturates 9 g

1 Place the herbs in a food processor and chop finely. Add the walnuts and process until they are reduced to very small pieces but not as small as crumbs.

2 Cook the pasta in boiling salted water and drain (see page 5), reserving a ladle of the cooking water for the sauce if necessary.

3 Stir in the oil, the nuts and herbs, the ricotta cheese and the Parmesan. If the pasta seems too dry, add a little pasta water. Season to taste and serve immediately.

COOK'S TIP

Ricotta is a soft, fragrant Italian cheese. Fresh ricotta cheese is unsalted with a delicate, smooth flavour which makes it very suitable for cooking.

FRESH PASTA WITH HERBS, TOMATO AND CHEESE

SERVES: 4　PREPARATION: 10 MINS　COOKING: 10 MINS

INGREDIENTS

3 tbsp olive oil

1 shallot or spring onion, peeled or
　trimmed and finely chopped

2 cloves garlic, peeled and finely
　chopped

3 ripe tomatoes, peeled, seeded and
　chopped into small cubes (see
　page 7)

500 g (1 lb) fresh pasta or
　pappardelle

salt and black pepper

2 tbsp fresh chopped herbs,
　including parsley, sage, rosemary
　and thyme

12 thin slices of fresh creamy goat's
　cheese

NUTRITION

Each portion contains:

Energy: 510 calories

Fat: 18 g of which saturates 7 g

1　Heat the oil and gently brown the shallot or spring onion and garlic. Add the tomato cubes and heat through.

2　Cook the pasta in boiling salted water (see page 5).

3　Stir the herbs into the tomato sauce and season while the pasta is cooking, leaving some for garnish.

4　Drain the pasta and stir in the sauce. Pour into individual serving bowls, arrange the cheese on top and dust with the remaining herbs. Pour on a few drops of olive oil, season with black pepper and serve at once.

COOK'S TIP

If you are making your own pasta, roll it out thinly then cut into rough and uneven diamond shapes. If you are buying pappardelle, break them into uneven lengths before cooking.

PENNE WITH GREEN BEANS AND GORGONZOLA

SERVES: 4   PREPARATION: 5 MINS   COOKING: 10 MINS

INGREDIENTS

500 g (1 lb) green beans

salt and black pepper

500 g (1 lb) penne

75 g (2½ oz) butter, diced

50 g (1½ oz) freshly grated
    Parmesan cheese

150 g (5 oz) Gorgonzola cheese,
    diced

NUTRITION

Each portion contains:

Energy: 815 calories

Fat: 35 g of which saturales 21 g

1 Cook the beans in boiling salted water and drain while they are still firm and a good colour.

2 Cook the pasta in boiling salted water (see page 5), drain and stir in the butter and Parmesan cheese. Add a generous amount of black pepper.

3 Gently stir in the beans and then the Gorgonzola. Serve at once.

COOK'S TIP

Although this sauce works well with most pasta, it looks best if you choose a short variety and cut the beans into lengths that match the pasta.

SPAGHETTI WITH LEMON AND CHIVES

SERVES: 4   PREPARATION: 10 MINS   COOKING: 10 MINS

INGREDIENTS

2 large juicy lemons

25 blades of chives, chopped

2 tbsp chopped parsley

5 tbsp olive oil

salt and black pepper

500 g (1 lb) spaghetti

lemon wedges to serve (optional)

NUTRITION

Each portion contains:

Energy: 550 calories

Fat: 16 g of which saturates 2 g

1 Grate the zest from the lemons, taking care not to use the bitter white pith. Squeeze out the juice and briefly process the chives and parsley with the lemon zest, juice and 1 tbsp of the oil in a food processor. Season to taste.

2 Cook the pasta in boiling salted water (see page 5), drain, and stir in the remaining oil. When the oil has been absorbed, stir in the sauce, garnish with a lemon wedge and serve at once.

COOK'S TIP

If you wish, this simple pasta dish can be decorated with some threads of lemon peel.

SPAGHETTI WITH GARLIC

SERVES: 4   PREPARATION: 5 MINS   COOKING: 10 MINS

INGREDIENTS

12 cloves garlic, peeled

100 ml (3½ fl oz) olive oil

salt

500 g (1 lb) spaghetti

1 tbsp chopped parsley

NUTRITION

Each portion contains:

Energy: 590 calories

Fat: 20 g of which saturates 3 g

1 Dice the garlic into small, even cubes – do not use a garlic squeezer or mincer.

2 Heat the oil and fry the garlic until it begins to change colour and then use a slotted spoon to remove it immediately from the hot oil.

3 Cook the pasta in boiling salted water (see page 5), drain and stir in the oil, garlic and parsley. Serve immediately.

COOK'S TIP

This dish is simple and very inexpensive, but the secret lies in never taking your eyes off the garlic when it is cooking. It needs to be a pale creamy beige and a few seconds too long in the oil will spoil the flavour and give a bitter taste.

See full picture on page 22.

SPAGHETTI WITH SUN-DRIED TOMATOES

SERVES: 4 PREPARATION: 10 MINS COOKING: 15 MINS

INGREDIENTS

3⅓ tbsp olive oil

1 small onion, peeled and finely chopped

1 celery stick, trimmed and chopped

250 g (8 oz) sun-dried tomatoes, chopped

300 g (9½ oz) tinned tomatoes, chopped

salt and black pepper

500 g (1 lb) spaghetti

NUTRITION

Each portion contains:

Energy: 840 calories

Fat: 44 g of which saturates 6 g

1 Heat the oil and add the onion. When this is soft add the celery and sun-dried tomatoes. Stir and cook for about 5 minutes, then add the tinned tomatoes. Cook quickly over a high heat until you have a thick sauce. Season to taste, using salt with caution because the sun-dried tomatoes are usually quite salty.

2 Cook the pasta in boiling salted water (see page 5), drain and stir in the sauce. Serve immediately.

COOK'S TIP

Freshly grated Parmesan cheese can be served separately, if you wish.

See full picture on page 23.

PENNE WITH HAZELNUTS

SERVES: 4 PREPARATION: 5 MINS COOKING: 10 MINS

INGREDIENTS

3 tbsp olive oil

1 clove garlic, peeled

1 pinch ground chilli or cayenne
    pepper

125 g (4 oz) shelled hazelnuts,
    finely chopped

500 g (1 lb) penne

salt and black pepper

75 g (2½ oz) freshly grated
    Parmesan cheese

NUTRITION

Each portion contains:

Energy: 800 calories

Fat: 36 g of which saturates 7 g

1 Heat the oil, add the garlic clove and allow it to turn golden brown. Add the chilli and hazelnuts, cook for a few minutes, then remove the garlic.

2 Cook the pasta in boiling salted water (see page 5), drain and stir in the cheese and the nuts. If the pasta seems too dry, stir in a ladle of pasta water before serving. Season to taste and serve at once.

COOK'S TIP

Piedmont, in northern Italy, has many traditional recipes using hazelnuts. This is an unusual new pasta dish using the same ingredient.

TAGLIATELLE WITH LEEKS

SERVES: 4   PREPARATION: 10 MINS   COOKING: 20 MINS

INGREDIENTS

4 leeks

30 g (1 oz) butter

salt and black pepper

3 tbsp light vegetable stock

180 ml (6⅓ fl oz) cream

500 g (1 lb) tagliatelle

75 g (2½ oz) freshly grated
    Parmesan cheese

NUTRITION

Each portion contains:

Energy: 680 calories

Fat: 24 g of which saturates 14 g

1 Using only the white and light green parts of the leeks, chop into thin rings. Melt the butter and cook the leeks gently with a little freshly ground black pepper.

2 When the leeks are soft add the stock and cream and simmer gently for 20 minutes. Check the seasoning.

3 Cook the pasta in boiling salted water (see page 5), drain and stir in the leek sauce and Parmesan cheese. Serve at once.

TAGLIATELLE WITH MUSHROOM SAUCE

SERVES: 4   PREPARATION TIME: 10 MINS   COOKING: 10 MINS

INGREDIENTS

50 g (1½ oz) butter

1 tbsp olive oil

1 shallot or spring onion, peeled or
    trimmed and sliced

400 g (12 oz) mushrooms, sliced

salt and black pepper

1 tbsp chopped parsley

500 g (1 lb) green tagliatelle

NUTRITION

Each portion contains:

Energy: 560 calories

Fat: 16 g of which saturates 7 g

1 Heat the butter and oil and gently fry the shallot or spring onion until soft.

2 Add the mushrooms and cook on a low heat for a few minutes. Season to taste and add the parsley. Keep warm.

3 Cook the pasta in boiling salted water (see page 5). Drain and stir in the sauce. Serve at once.

COOK'S TIP

To clean the mushrooms, brush any soil off and wipe them clean with a damp cloth. Do not wash by immersing them in water or you will ruin the taste and texture of the mushrooms.

HERB RAVIOLI FILLED WITH TOMATO AND MOZZARELLA

SERVES: 6 AS A STARTER

PREPARATION: 20 MINS, PLUS STANDING TIME COOKING: 10 MINS

INGREDIENTS

For the filling:

100 g (3½ oz) tomatoes, peeled, de-seeded and finely chopped (see page 7)

100 g (3½ oz) mozzarella cheese, diced

1 tbsp basil leaves cut into fine strips

salt and black pepper

For the pasta:

3 eggs

30 g (1 oz) butter, melted

2 cloves garlic, peeled and finely chopped

1 tbsp finely chopped rosemary

1 tbsp finely chopped thyme

salt and black pepper

450 g (14½ oz) strong plain flour

50 g (1½ oz) butter, melted

50 g (1½ oz) freshly grated Parmesan cheese

12 sprigs basil for decoration

1 To make the filling, mix together all the ingredients. Let the mixture stand for about 1 hour to allow the flavours to blend. Season to taste.

2 To make the pasta, beat the eggs and add the melted butter, garlic, herbs and seasoning. Gradually work in the flour, adding a little water if necessary. Roll out the pasta to a sheet 5 mm (⅕ in) thick and cut out 12 large squares about 10 x 8 cm (4 x 3 in). This will give one giant ravioli per serving. Cover the pasta while you are making the filling.

3 Arrange the filling on six squares and cover with the remaining squares, sealing the edges well. Cook in boiling salted water for about 10 minutes. Lift out with a slotted spoon and dress with melted butter and cheese. Arrange 2 sprigs of basil on top of each ravioli. Serve at once.

NUTRITION

Each portion contains:

Energy: 490 calories

Fat: 21 g of which saturates 12 g

COOK'S TIP

Here a combination of fresh herbs makes an interesting pasta dough that can be used with many fillings. It gives an original flavour to the long-time favourite tomato and mozzarella.

AUBERGINE BOATS STUFFED WITH PASTA

SERVES: 6 AS A STARTER

PREPARATION: 15 MINS, PLUS DRAINING TIME   COOKING: 20 MINS

INGREDIENTS

6 plump aubergines

salt and black pepper

2 tbsp olive oil

750 ml (1¼ pt) fresh tomato sauce
    (see page 9)

vegetable oil, for frying the
    aubergine casing

400 g (12 oz) small pasta tubes,
    such as rigatoni

100 g (3½ oz) mozzarella cheese,
    diced

100 g (3½ oz) freshly grated
    Parmesan cheese

12 basil leaves for decoration

NUTRITION

Each portion contains:

Energy: 550 calories

Fat: 25 g of which saturates 9 g

1 Cut the stalks off the aubergines, lay them lengthwise and slice off the top third of each. Cut this top third into cubes.

2 Using a curved knife, carve out the flesh from the larger segments, being careful not to spoil the shape or cut the skin. Chop the flesh into small cubes, and mix them with the rest of the aubergine cubes. Cover with salt for 30 minutes to draw out the bitter juice. Rinse off the salt and pat dry.

3 Heat the oil and gently cook the diced aubergine for 5 minutes. Add the tomato sauce and keep warm.

4 In enough oil to coat the pan, fry the aubergine 'shells' with the skin upwards so that they are pliable without being too soft to handle. Cool on paper towels to remove any excess oil.

5 Preheat the oven to 240°C/475°F/gas 9. Place the pasta in boiling salted water, then remove from the heat while it is still slightly undercooked and drain. Stir in the mozzarella, the sauce and the Parmesan cheese. Spoon the mixture into the aubergine casings, place on a baking tray and bake for 5–10 minutes. Decorate with the basil leaves then serve at once.

See full picture on page 35.

PASTA SHELLS WITH VEGETABLES

SERVES: 4   PREPARATION: 15 MINS, PLUS DRAINING TIME

COOKING: 15 MINS

INGREDIENTS

2 medium-sized aubergines, diced

3 tbsp olive oil

1 onion, peeled and finely chopped

2 cloves garlic, peeled and finely
   chopped

5 ripe tomatoes, peeled, de-seeded
   and chopped (see page 7)

salt and black pepper

150 g (5 oz) small green beans

1 sweet green pepper and 1 sweet
   yellow pepper, de-seeded and
   cut into small pieces

pinch of dried oregano

500 g (1 lb) conchiglie pasta shells

50 g (1½ oz) freshly grated
   Parmesan cheese

NUTRITION

Each portion contains:

Energy: 630 calories

Fat: 17 g of which saturates 4 g

1 Place the diced aubergine on a plate, cover with salt and leave for
   1 hour to drain its bitter liquid. Rinse off the salt and pat dry.

2 Heat half the oil and gently cook the onion, garlic, tomatoes and
   aubergine. Season to taste.

3 Cook the beans in boiling salted water until they are not quite tender.

4 Heat the remaining oil and cook the sweet peppers with the oregano
   and a little salt until almost tender. Mix the drained beans with all
   the other vegetables and cook for 5 minutes.

5 Cook the pasta in boiling salted water (see page 5), drain and stir in
   the Parmesan and vegetables. Serve at once.

COOK'S TIP

If you wish, the fresh tomatoes
can be replaced with the same
weight of drained tinned tomatoes.

See full picture on page 34.

PENNE WITH ONIONS AND PARMESAN

SERVES: 4   PREPARATION: 5 MINS   COOKING: 10 MINS

INGREDIENTS

100 g (3½ oz) butter

2 very large onions, peeled and
    finely chopped

salt and black pepper

500 g (1 lb) penne

3 eggs, beaten

125 g (4 oz) freshly grated
    Parmesan cheese

NUTRITION

Each portion contains:

Energy: 850 calories

Fat: 38 g of which saturates 22 g

1 Melt the butter and cook the onions slowly over a low heat until they are almost transparent. Do not let the onions change colour. Season to taste and keep warm.

2 Cook the pasta in boiling salted water (see page 5).

3 When the pasta is nearly ready, return the onions to a low heat and stir in the beaten eggs. Remove from the heat. Drain the pasta and quickly stir in the cheese and the onion sauce. Serve at once.

COOK'S TIP

This is a deliciously different pasta which provides instant comfort on a cold day. It goes very well with a fine robust red wine, such as Chianti.

PASTA FRITTERS

SERVES: 4   PREPARATION: 5 MINS   COOKING: 15 MINS

INGREDIENTS

500 g (1 lb) angel's hair pasta

150 g (5 oz) freshly grated
     Parmesan cheese

75 g (2½ oz) butter, melted

30 g (1 oz) mushrooms, finely
     chopped

3 eggs

salt and black pepper

vegetable oil for frying

NUTRITION

Each portion contains:

Energy: 816 calories

Fat: 40 g of which saturates 20 g

1 Cook the pasta in boiling salted water and drain (see page 5). Stir in the cheese, melted butter and mushrooms.

2 Beat the eggs with a little salt and pepper and stir them into the pasta mixture.

3 Pour enough oil into a frying pan to cover the base. Heat the oil until hot. With a fork, make little tangles of pasta, about the size of a large walnut. Drop these little pasta balls into the hot oil and fry until golden. Drain on paper towels and serve at once.

COOK'S TIP

You can use many different ingredients in these crisp little fritters – try replacing the mushrooms with chopped ham. They can even be made with leftover pasta, but are most effective made with very thin pasta. They also make unusual nibbles to serve with drinks before dinner.

LINGUINE DEVIL'S FASHION

SERVES: 4   PREPARATION: 15 MINS   COOKING: 15 MINS

INGREDIENTS

3 tbsp olive oil

1 onion, peeled and chopped

2 cloves garlic, peeled and chopped

1 hot red chilli pepper

6 large sweet red peppers,
    de-seeded and roughly chopped

3 ripe tomatoes, fresh or tinned,
    chopped

salt and black pepper

cayenne pepper, to taste (optional)

500 g (1 lb) linguine

NUTRITION

Each portion contains:

Energy: 600 calories

Fat: 12 g of which saturates 2 g

1 Heat the oil and gently cook the onion and garlic. As they begin to change colour, add the chilli, red peppers and tomatoes.

2 Cook until the vegetables are soft, remove the chilli and then blend the vegetables in a food processor or blender. Check the seasoning and add a little cayenne pepper if the sauce is too bland.

3 Cook the pasta in boiling salted water (see page 5), drain and stir in the sauce. Serve at once.

COOK'S TIP

This pasta gets its devilish name from the very small hot red chillies known as *diavolicchi* or little devils.

PUMPKIN GNOCCHI

SERVES: 4 PREPARATION: 10 MINS, PLUS CHILLING TIME

COOKING: 1 HOUR 10 MINS

INGREDIENTS

1 kg (2 lb) fresh pumpkin, cut into
    large pieces
250 g (8 oz) plain flour
30 g (1 oz) freshly grated Parmesan
    cheese
1 large egg
salt and black pepper
30 g (1 oz) butter, melted
30 g (1 oz) freshly grated Parmesan
    cheese
pinch of nutmeg

NUTRITION

Each portion contains:

Energy: 300 calories

Fat: 5 g of which saturates 2 g

1 Preheat the oven to 160ºC/325ºF/gas 3. Place the pumpkin pieces on a baking tray and cook for an hour in the oven. When the pumpkin is cooked and fairly dry, remove any peel and seeds, then purée the flesh in a blender or food processor. If the pulp seems too liquid, reduce it by boiling over a high heat.

2 Put 450 g (14½ oz) of the pulp in a bowl and stir in the flour, cheese, egg and seasoning. Let the mixture stand in the refrigerator for at least half an hour.

3 Bring a wide, shallow pan of water to a brisk boil. Add salt and then drop in spoonfuls of the pumpkin mixture. The gnocchi are cooked when they float to the surface. Remove them quickly with a slotted spoon and serve at once, covered with melted butter, freshly grated Parmesan and a little grated nutmeg.

COOK'S TIP

Gnocchi are most often made with potato, but this tasty and colourful variation uses chunks of fresh pumpkin instead.

SPINACH GNOCCHI WITH BEAN SAUCE

SERVES: 4   PREPARATION: 15 MINS, PLUS SOAKING TIME

COOKING: 30 MINS, PLUS TIME FOR BAKING THE POTATOES

INGREDIENTS

For the gnocchi:

400 g (12 oz) floury (baking)
    potatoes

300 g (9½ oz) spinach leaves,
    chopped

180 g (6 oz) plain flour

1 egg yolk

pinch of nutmeg

salt

For the sauce:

150 g (5 oz) dried haricot (navy)
    beans, soaked for 12 hours

100 g (3½ oz) butter

3 leeks, sliced into thin rings

salt and black pepper

12 basil leaves

NUTRITION

Each portion contains:

Energy: 570 calories

Fat: 24 g of which saturates 14 g

1   To make the gnocchi, bake the potatoes in their skins. Remove the skins while still hot and mash the potatoes. Boil the spinach leaves until wilted, drain very thoroughly and add the potatoes. Stir in the flour, egg yolk and seasoning. When the mixture is quite cool, roll it into thin cylinders and cut into 2 cm (¾ in) lengths. Set aside while you make the sauce.

2   To make the sauce, drain the beans and cook until tender in boiling salted water. Melt half the butter and cook the leeks gently with a little salt and black pepper. When the leeks are soft, add the basil leaves, cover and remove from the heat. Drain the beans and stir them into the leeks.

3   Cook the gnocchi in boiling salted water for about 3 minutes. When they float to the top, lift them out with a slotted spoon and transfer to a serving dish. Melt the remaining butter and pour over the gnocchi. Gently stir in the sauce and serve at once.

PASTA
with seafood

TAGLIOLINI WITH CITRUS PEEL AND PRAWNS

SERVES: 4   PREPARATION: 15 MINS   COOKING: 10 MINS

INGREDIENTS

3 lemons

3 oranges

100 ml (3½ fl oz) olive oil

300 g (9½ oz) prawns, shelled with central vein removed (leave the tails on for decoration if you wish)

salt

600 g (1 lb 31/2 oz) tagliolini

NUTRITION

Each portion contains:

Energy: 750 calories

Fat: 22 g of which saturates 3 g

1 Remove the peel from the lemons and oranges, taking care to avoid the bitter white pith. Cut the peel into very fine strips. The whole process can be done very successfully using a sharp zesting tool.

2 Heat the oil and gently cook the prawns for 3 minutes.

3 Quickly cook the pasta in boiling water (see page 5). Drain the pasta while it is still very much al dente and stir it into the pan with the prawns. Add the lemon and orange peel and serve at once.

COOK'S TIP

Fresh tagliolini will cook in a few minutes, and even the dry variety cooks quickly. You could replace the tagliolini with the slightly wider tagliatelle if you wish, but it will take a little longer to cook.

PENNE WITH ASPARAGUS AND RED MULLET

SERVES: 6   PREPARATION: 15 MINS   COOKING: 15 MINS

INGREDIENTS

400 g (12 oz) green asparagus
   spears
6 red mullet, cut into fillets, skin
   left on
100 g (3½ oz) butter
salt and black pepper
500 g (1 lb) penne

NUTRITION

Each portion contains:

Energy: 590 calories

Fat: 21 g of which saturates 9 g

1   Cut the tips from the asparagus and keep to one side. Cut the tender parts of the stalks in 2 cm (¾ in) lengths. Discard the woody parts of the stalks.

2   Keep six fillets of fish whole and cut the other six into thin strips. Melt a third of the butter and gently cook the whole fish fillets. After 5 minutes add the asparagus tips. Season to taste. Cook for a further few minutes until tender then cover and keep warm.

3   Melt half the remaining butter, cook the fish strips until done and season to taste. Cook the asparagus stalks in boiling salted water until tender, drain then add to the fish strips.

4   Cook the pasta in boiling salted water (see page 5), drain and gently stir in the fish strips and asparagus stalks. Serve on a large heated plate with the whole fillets and asparagus tips arranged decoratively on top.

COOK'S TIP

You can use any delicate white fish (such as snapper or trout) if red mullet is not available.

TAGLIATELLE WITH SHELLFISH AND SWEET PEPPERS

SERVES: 4   PREPARATION: 10 MINS   COOKING: 20 MINS

INGREDIENTS

1 kg (2 lb) mixed seafood, such as
    mussels and clams

salt and black pepper

5 tbsp olive oil

1 sweet yellow pepper, de-seeded
    and cut into fine strips

1 sweet red pepper, de-seeded and
    cut into fine strips

500 g (1 lb) tagliatelle

NUTRITION

Each portion contains:

Energy: 650 calories

Fat: 18 g of which saturates 3 g

1 Scrub and wash the shellfish well to remove the grit. Discard any broken or open shells. Cover with lightly salted water and cook over a high heat until the shells open. Drain, reserve the cooking liquid to add to the pasta water and discard any closed shellfish. Remove the shellfish from their shells and keep warm.

2 In a large pan or wok heat the oil and cook the peppers for 10 minutes. Add the shellfish, 100 ml (3½ fl oz) of the shellfish cooking liquid and season to taste.

3 Cook the pasta in boiling salted water to which the remaining shellfish cooking water has been added (see page 5). Drain and stir into the sauce. Simmer for another 2 minutes then serve at once.

COOK'S TIP

The combination of colourful sweet peppers and mixed shellfish makes this a memorable pasta dish. If you wish, some of the cooked seafood can be left in the shells as a decorative garnish. Alternatively, you could use a bag of frozen mixed seafood – simply thaw and drain, then cook as instructed on the packet.

TAGLIATELLE WITH SCALLOPS AND FENNEL

SERVES: 6 PREPARATION: 15 MINS COOKING: 20 MINS

INGREDIENTS

3 young, tender fennel bulbs, tough
  tubes and outer leaves removed,
  thinly sliced

4 tbsp olive oil

2 cloves garlic, peeled and finely
  chopped

2 shallots or spring onions,peeled
  or trimmed and finely chopped

150 ml (5 fl oz) dry white wine

12 or 18 scallops (2 or 3 per
  serving, depending on their size
  and how rich you want to make
  the dish), shelled, washed and
  dried

salt and pepper

500 g (1 lb) tagliatelle

1 tbsp chopped parsley

NUTRITION

Each portion contains:

Energy: 440 calories

Fat: 10 g of which saturates 2 g

1 Steam the fennel slices by placing them in a colander over a saucepan of water and covering with a lid until they are nearly soft.

2 Heat half the oil in a large pan or wok and add the garlic. As it begins to change colour, add the steamed fennel slices and keep warm so the flavours mingle.

3 Heat the remaining oil in a frying pan and add the shallots or spring onions. Stir and fry them until they become soft, then add the scallops. Cook for a few minutes then pour in the wine. Reduce the sauce over a high heat until it thickens slightly and season to taste.

4 Cook the tagliatelle in boiling salted water (see page 5), drain and stir into the pan with the fennel. Cook for another minute then check seasoning and stir in the parsley. Serve the pasta at once, arranging the scallops and their sauce on top of each portion.

TAGLIATELLE WITH PRAWNS AND MUSHROOMS

SERVES: 4   PREPARATION: 10 MINS   COOKING: 15 MINS

INGREDIENTS

2 tbsp olive oil

1 clove garlic, peeled and crushed

300 g (9½ oz) mushrooms, sliced

salt and black pepper

3 ripe tomatoes, peeled, de-seeded
 and chopped (see page 7)

300 g (9½ oz) prawns, shelled with
 central vein removed (leave the
 tails on for decoration if you
 wish)

3 tbsp dry white wine

500 g (1 lb) tagliatelle

1 tbsp chopped parsley, to garnish

NUTRITION

Each portion contains:

Energy: 570 calories

Fat: 9 g of which saturates 1 g

1 Heat half the oil and add the garlic clove. Let the garlic become golden brown before removing it with a spoon and discarding it. Add the sliced mushrooms to the oil and cook gently for about 10 minutes. Season to taste, then add the chopped tomatoes.

2 Heat the remaining oil in another pan and quickly toss the prawns in it. Season. Cook for 1 minute, then pour in the wine. Let the wine evaporate over a high heat, then stir in the mushrooms and tomatoes.

3 Cook the pasta in boiling salted water (see page 5), drain and stir in the sauce. Sprinkle with parsley and serve at once.

See full picture on page 58.

PASTA WITH ANCHOVIES

SERVES: 4   PREPARATION: 10 MINS   COOKING: 15 MINS

INGREDIENTS

12 anchovy fillets in oil

3 cloves garlic, peeled and chopped

2 tbsp chopped parsley

3 tbsp olive oil

salt and black pepper

100 g (3½ oz) breadcrumbs

500 g (1 lb) spaghetti

25 g (1 oz) pine nuts, lightly
  toasted

25 g (1 oz) sultanas, lightly toasted

NUTRITION

Each portion contains:

Energy: 670 calories

Fat: 17 g of which saturates 2 g

1 Remove the anchovy fillets from their oil, break them up and mash them with a few drops of water to make a smooth paste. Add the garlic, parsley and two-thirds of the oil, stir and season to taste. Set aside.

2 Heat a heavy-based pan and lightly toast the breadcrumbs before adding the remaining oil in a fine thread. Stir the breadcrumbs so that they are coated in oil, then cover and keep them warm.

3 Cook the pasta in boiling salted water (see page 5), drain and stir in the anchovy sauce. If the pasta seems too dry, add a little of the pasta cooking water to the sauce. Decorate the individual servings with sprinklings of breadcrumbs, pine nuts and sultanas.

COOK'S TIP

This recipe comes from Franca Colonna Romano's book on Sicilian cooking. She explains that in Sicilian this dish is humorously called 'pasta with the sardines at sea' because it is made with canned anchovies which leaves the sardines still swimming in the sea.

See full picture on page 59.

FUSILLI WITH MUSSELS AND POTATOES

SERVES: 4   PREPARATION: 15 MINS   COOKING: 20 MINS

INGREDIENTS

500 g (1 lb) mussels

salt

250 g (8 oz) potatoes

100 ml (3½ fl oz) olive oil

500 g (1 lb) fusilli or penne

1 red chilli pepper

4 cloves garlic, peeled and finely
    chopped

1 tbsp chopped parsley

NUTRITION

Each portion contains:

Energy: 680 calories

Fat: 21 g of which saturates 3 g

1 Wash the mussels well under running water to remove the grit, then scrape them clean, discarding any broken or open shells. Cover with lightly salted water and cook over a high heat until the shells open. Remove the mussels from their shells, discarding any that fail to open spontaneously. Strain and reserve the cooking liquid to add to the pasta water.

2 Peel the potatoes and boil in salted water until they are nearly cooked. They should not be allowed to get too soft. Cut into slices, then into sticks about 1 cm (⅓ in) wide.

3 Heat half the oil in a pan and add the mussels and potatoes. Cook for 5 minutes and then add 3 tbsp of the mussel liquid. Keep warm.

4 Cook the pasta in boiling salted water combined with the rest of the mussel liquid (see page 5). Heat the remaining oil and cook the chilli pepper and garlic until golden brown. Discard the chilli. Drain the pasta and stir into the mussels and potatoes. Add the parsley to the pasta, cook for a few minutes then pour on the garlic and oil. Serve at once.

COOK'S TIP

If you wish, leave some cooked mussels in their shells to add a decorative touch to this south Italian dish or you could replace the fresh mussels with two small tins of mussels.

SPAGHETTI WITH ANCHOVIES AND ORANGE SAUCE

SERVES: 4   PREPARATION: 15 MINS   COOKING: 10 MINS

INGREDIENTS

200 g (6½ oz) anchovy fillets in oil

2 tbsp olive oil

1 clove garlic, peeled and finely
    chopped

2 oranges

1 tbsp fresh breadcrumbs

50 ml (3⅓ tbsp) orange liqueur
    such as Grand Marnier

salt

500 g (1 lb) spaghetti

1 tbsp chopped mint

NUTRITION

Each portion contains:

Energy: 690 calories

Fat: 18 g of which saturates 1 g

1   Cut the anchovies into pieces.

2   Heat the oil and add the garlic. When the garlic begins to change colour add the anchovies and push with a wooden spoon until they 'melt' and form a thick cream.

3   Remove the peel, including the white pith, from the oranges and cut it into little cubes. Add these orange cubes to the anchovies with the breadcrumbs and the liqueur. Add salt if necessary.

4   Cook the pasta in boiling salted water (see page 5), drain and stir in the sauce. Sprinkle with chopped mint and serve at once.

SPAGHETTI WITH SALMON

SERVES: 4 PREPARATION: 10 MINS, PLUS MARINATING TIME

COOKING: 10 MINS

INGREDIENTS

250 g (8 oz) smoked salmon, cut
  into small strips

3 tbsp lemon juice

4 tbsp olive oil

2 teaspoons chopped wild fennel or
  dill

salt and black pepper

1 clove garlic, peeled

500 g (1 lb) spaghetti

NUTRITION

Each portion contains:

Energy: 760 calories

Fat: 28 g of which saturates 4 g

1 Put the salmon in a bowl and cover with the lemon juice, half the oil, the herbs and seasoning. Leave to marinate for at least an hour.

2 When ready to serve heat the remaining oil, add the garlic clove and when it turns a golden brown remove it from the pan and discard.

3 Cook the pasta in boiling salted water (see page 5), drain and stir into the warm garlic oil. Drain the salmon, keeping some of the marinade to dress the pasta if it seems too dry. Stir in the salmon and serve at once.

COOK'S TIP

Try serving this dish cold in the summer. Plunge the pasta into cold water after cooking, drain again then stir into the cooled, aromatic garlic oil. Add the salmon just before serving.

SPAGHETTI WITH BROCCOLI AND CLAMS

SERVES: 4   PREPARATION: 15 MINS   COOKING: 20 MINS

INGREDIENTS

1 kg (2 lb) broccoli, divided into
    florets

salt

2 tbsp olive oil

5 cloves garlic, all peeled,
    1 chopped and 4 whole

2 red chilli peppers

1 kg (2 lb) clams in their shells,
    rinsed and scrubbed

150 ml (5 fl oz) dry white wine

1 tbsp chopped parsley

500 g (1 lb) spaghetti

NUTRITION

Each portion contains:

Energy: 650 calories

Fat: 11 g of which saturates 2 g

1 Cook the broccoli in boiling salted water until half done. Drain and keep the broccoli water for the pasta.

2 Heat half the oil and add the chopped garlic clove and one whole chilli pepper. When they begin to change colour, add the shellfish and turn up the heat. After a few minutes pour in the white wine and remove the chilli. Remove the clams, reserving the cooking liquid, and take them out of their shells. Discard any clams where the shells have not opened. Set aside, cover and keep warm.

3 Heat the remaining oil and add the four whole garlic cloves and the other chilli pepper. When they begin to change colour, add the broccoli. Let the broccoli cook for a few minutes to absorb the flavours, then discard the garlic and chilli pepper. Pour in the stock from the shellfish and cook for a few minutes. Add the parsley.

4 Cook the pasta in the boiling broccoli liquid, adding more water if necessary (see page 5). Drain and stir in the shellfish and broccoli. Serve at once.

COOK'S TIP

This recipe works equally well with mussels in place of clams. You could also use tinned clams instead of fresh ones. If you wish, retain some of the seafood shells as a decorative garnish.

SPAGHETTI WITH TUNA AND LENTILS

SERVES: 4   PREPARATION: 10 MINS, PLUS SOAKING TIME

COOKING: 25 MINS

INGREDIENTS

300 g (9½ oz) dried continental
(green or brown) lentils

3⅓ tbsp olive oil

1 carrot, peeled and finely chopped

1 onion, peeled and finely chopped

1 stick celery, trimmed and finely
chopped

300 g (9½ oz) canned tuna in oil,
drained

1 tbsp chopped parsley

salt and black pepper

500 g (1 lb) spaghetti

NUTRITION

Each portion contains:

Energy content: 890 calories

Fat content: 20 g of which saturates 3 g

1 Soak the dried lentils in water for 5–6 hours, then drain.

2 Heat half the oil in a pan and add the vegetables. Stir and fry them for 1–2 minutes, then add the lentils. Add plenty of boiling salted water and cook the lentils until soft – they usually take about 25 minutes.

3 Drain the lentils and mix them in a bowl with the tuna, parsley, salt, pepper and remaining oil.

4 Cook the pasta in boiling salted water (see page 5), drain and stir in the sauce. Serve at once.

COOK'S TIP

This healthy, inexpensive pasta can be made from the ingredients to be found in most store cupboards. Tuna in olive oil makes a tastier sauce than tuna in brine, and canned lentils can be used to save time.

RIGATONI STUFFED WITH FISH

SERVES: 4   PREPARATION: 15 MINS, PLUS MARINATING TIME

COOKING: 15 MINS

INGREDIENTS

300 g (9½ oz) fish fillets

5 tbsp olive oil

juice of 1 lemon

2 cloves garlic, peeled and crushed

2 carrots, peeled and finely chopped

1 medium onion, peeled and finely
     chopped

1 tbsp finely chopped parsley

salt and black pepper

500 g (1 lb) rigatoni

30 g (1 oz) breadcrumbs

500 ml (16 fl oz) fresh tomato
     sauce (see page 9)

50 g (1½ oz) freshly grated
     Parmesan cheese

NUTRITION

Each portion contains:

Energy: 840 calories

Fat: 28 g of which saturates 7 g

1 Cover the fish fillets with 4 tbsp of the oil, lemon juice, garlic, carrot, onion, parsley and salt, cover and leave in the fridge for at least 2 hours. Drain off the liquid and process the fish and vegetables in a blender or food processor to form a dense cream.

2 Cook the pasta in boiling salted water until pliable, not soft (see page 5), drain and fill with the fish mixture, using a pastry bag and a wide nozzle.

3 Preheat the oven to 200°C/400°F/gas 6. Lightly oil a large ovenproof dish with the remaining oil, arrange the rigatoni and cover with breadcrumbs. Pour on the tomato sauce, sprinkle with grated cheese and pepper, then cook in the oven until golden brown. Serve at once.

COOK'S TIP

Any readily available, inexpensive fish can be used in this recipe. Ask the fish counter in your supermarket for advice.

LINGUINE WITH FISH BALLS

SERVES: 4   PREPARATION: 20 MINS   COOKING: 15 MINS

INGREDIENTS

100 g (3½ oz) stale white bread
   with crusts removed

milk to soak bread

fish fillets weighing about 700 g
   (1½ lb)

2 eggs, separated

50 g (1½ oz) butter, melted

100 g (3½ oz) freshly grated
   Parmesan cheese

salt and black pepper

3 tbsp olive oil

1 onion, peeled and finely chopped

400 g (12 oz) can plum tomatoes,
   chopped

500 g (1 lb) linguine

NUTRITION

Each portion contains:

Energy: 980 calories

Fat: 34 g of which saturates 15 g

1 Soak the bread in a little milk to soften, then squeeze out the excess milk.

2 Put the fish, egg yolks, melted butter, cheese and bread in a blender or food processor and blend to a smooth paste. Add salt and pepper.

3 Whisk the egg whites until stiff and gently fold them into the fish paste. Shape the mixture into little balls about the size of a walnut.

4 Heat the oil in a medium-sized saucepan, gently cook the onion then add the tomatoes. Squash the tomatoes with a wooden spoon then gently drop in the fish balls and allow them to simmer gently for about 15 minutes until cooked.

5 Cook the pasta in boiling salted water (see page 5), drain and stir in the sauce and fish balls. Serve at once.

COOK'S TIP

This is a fishy version of the old standby, spaghetti and meat balls. Any firm-fleshed fish, such as cod, can be used.

LINGUINE WITH SARDINES

SERVES: 4   PREPARATION: 10 MINS   COOKING: 10 MINS

INGREDIENTS

3 tbsp olive oil

2 cloves garlic, peeled and chopped

8 sardines in oil, drained and
    chopped

5 anchovy fillets in oil, drained and
    chopped

juice of 2 lemons

salt and black pepper

500 g (1 lb) linguine

1 tbsp chopped parsley

NUTRITION

Each portion contains:

Energy: 630 calories

Fat: 18 g of which saturates 3 g

1 Heat the oil, add the garlic and when it begins to change colour add the sardines and anchovies. Cook gently until the sardines and anchovies 'melt' and you have a thick paste. Stir in the lemon juice and check the seasoning.

2 Cook the pasta in boiling salted water (see page 5), drain and stir in the sauce. Sprinkle with parsley and serve at once.

COOK'S TIP

This is a very quick and easy recipe that can be made with not much more than a couple of cans from the pantry.

PASTA
with meat

FETTUCCINE WITH CHICKEN AND SWEET PEPPERS

SERVES: 4   PREPARATION: 15 MINS   COOKING: 25 MINS

INGREDIENTS

3 sweet peppers – red, yellow and
    green
2 tbsp olive oil
1 onion, peeled and chopped
2 cloves garlic, peeled and chopped
1 chicken, boned and cut into small
    pieces
2 tbsp dry white wine
1 tbsp concentrated tomato paste
100 ml (3½ fl oz) light chicken
    stock
salt and black pepper
500 g (1 lb) fettuccine

NUTRITION

Each portion contains:
Energy: 855 calories
Fat: 19 g of which saturates 5 g

1 Pre-heat the oven to its highest setting. Place the peppers on a baking tray and roast in the oven until the skin blisters and can be easily removed. (You can omit this step but peeling does make the peppers more digestible.) Cut the peppers into strips.

2 Heat the oil and gently brown the chopped onion and garlic. Add the chicken pieces and brown them on all sides. Pour in the wine and the tomato paste diluted with a little light stock. Add the peppers and simmer gently for about 25 minutes to obtain a thick sauce. Add a little more stock if the sauce becomes too dry. Season to taste.

3 Cook the pasta in boiling salted water (see page 5), drain, and stir in the sauce. Serve at once.

COOK'S TIP

Rome is famous for its savoury chicken and sweet pepper casserole and this recipe uses the same winning combination in a robust pasta dish which can make a one-dish meal if desired.

BAKED CAPELLINI WITH HAM AND MOZZARELLA

SERVES: 4–6 PREPARATION: 10 MINS COOKING: 15 MINS

INGREDIENTS

50 g (1½ oz) breadcrumbs

3 eggs

salt and black pepper

500 g (1 lb) capellini (see Cook's Tip)

100 g (3½ oz) freshly grated Parmesan cheese

100 g (3½ oz) butter, melted

150 g (5 oz) Parma ham, thinly sliced

300 g (9½ oz) mozzarella cheese, thinly sliced

NUTRITION

Each portion contains:

Energy: 770–1150 calories

Fat: 38–56 g of which saturates 21–32 g

1 Butter a shallow ovenproof dish and sprinkle with half the breadcrumbs.

2 Beat the eggs with a little salt and pepper.

3 Cook the pasta in boiling salted water (see page 5), drain, and stir in three-quarters of the Parmesan cheese and three-quarters of the butter.

4 Pre-heat the oven to 240°C/475°F/gas 9. Put half the pasta into the ovenproof dish and cover with the ham and mozzarella cheese slices. Pour over the eggs and then add the rest of the pasta. Sprinkle with the remaining breadcrumbs, Parmesan and butter. Bake in the oven until golden brown. Serve at once.

COOK'S TIP

Any pasta can be used to make this recipe but it works best with thin pasta. Capellini are thin strands of pasta, sometimes sold in nests. Most of the recipe can be prepared in advance, then finished off with the topping and cooked just before you eat.

ORECCHIETTE WITH LAMB SAUCE

SERVES: 4–6   PREPARATION: 10 MINS   COOKING: 30 MINS

INGREDIENTS

2 tbsp olive oil

100 g (3½ oz) butter

spikes from 1 sprig of rosemary

1 kg (2 lb) lamb, boned and cut
    into small pieces

salt and black pepper

500 g (1 lb) orecchiette or short
    concave pasta

75 g (2½ oz) freshly grated
    Parmesan cheese

NUTRITION

Each portion contains:

Energy: 770–1150 calories

Fat: 38–56 g of which saturates 19–29 g

1 Heat the oil and butter, add the rosemary and the lamb. Brown the pieces of meat on all sides. Season to taste, cover and cook slowly for about 30 minutes or until the meat is tender, adding a little water from time to time. Do not add too much water because the sauce should be thick. When the meat is cooked, put it aside while you prepare the pasta.

2 Cook the pasta in boiling salted water (see page 5), drain and serve with the meat sauce. The freshly grated Parmesan is served separately.

COOK'S TIP

These little disk-shaped flour and water pasta are a speciality of southern Italy.
They are also known as 'little ears'.

FETTUCCINE WITH CHICKEN LIVERS

SERVES: 4   PREPARATION: 10 MINS   COOKING: 10 MINS

INGREDIENTS

100 g (3½ oz) butter

1 clove garlic, peeled and finely
    chopped

200 g (6½ oz) cleaned chicken
    livers, diced

4 sage leaves, finely chopped, plus
    some whole leaves to garnish

1 sprig rosemary, finely chopped

salt and black pepper

500 g (1 lb) fettuccine

75 g (2½ oz) freshly grated
    Parmesan cheese

NUTRITION

Each portion contains:

Energy: 750 calories

Fat: 32 g of which saturates 10 g

1 Heat the butter and add the garlic. When it begins to change colour, add the chicken livers and herbs. Season to taste and cook gently until the chicken livers are cooked through but still tender.

2 Cook the pasta in boiling salted water (see page 5), drain, and toss in the cheese before stirring in the sauce. Decorate with whole sage leaves and serve at once.

COOK'S TIP

In this recipe a combination of chicken livers and herbs is used to make a tasty, filling pasta dish. Although it is traditionally made with wide ribbons of pappardelle, I prefer to use the thinner fettuccine.

BAKED RIGATONI WITH FENNEL, CREAM AND HAM

SERVES: 4   PREPARATION: 10 MINS   COOKING: 40 MINS

INGREDIENTS

500 g (1 lb) fennel bulbs

salt and black pepper

100 ml (3½ fl oz) fresh cream

2 tbsp olive oil

30 g (1 oz) butter

150 g (5 oz) cooked ham, diced

500 g (1 lb) rigatoni

50 g (1½ oz) freshly grated
   Parmesan cheese

NUTRITION

Each portion contains:

Energy: 700 calories

Fat: 23 g of which saturates 11 g

1 Remove the feathery tubes and any tough fibres from the fennel. Roughly chop two-thirds into slices and cook until tender in lightly salted boiling water. Drain and purée in a blender or food processor. Stir in the cream and season to taste.

2 Cut the remaining fennel into small cubes and cook gently in the oil and butter for 15 minutes, then add the diced ham. Season to taste.

3 Pre-heat the oven to 200°C/400°F/gas 6. Half-cook the pasta in boiling salted water (see page 5), drain and stir in the cream sauce, followed by the ham and fennel mixture. Turn into a shallow greased ovenproof dish and sprinkle with the freshly grated Parmesan cheese. Add some black pepper and cook in the oven for 15–20 minutes. Serve at once.

COOK'S TIP
This pasta can be prepared in advance and stored, covered, in the fridge and put in the oven just before you are ready to eat.

MOULDED PASTA WITH MEAT, CHEESE AND AUBERGINE

SERVES: 4–6 PREPARATION: 15 MINS, PLUS DRAINING TIME

COOKING: 50 MINS, PLUS STANDING TIME

INGREDIENTS

2 large aubergines

salt and black pepper

2 tbsp olive oil

2 cloves garlic, peeled and finely
    chopped

150 g (5 oz) lean pork or veal,
    chopped

500 ml (16 fl oz) fresh tomato
    sauce (see page 9)

vegetable oil, for deep frying
    aubergines

500 g (1 lb) rigatoni

200 g (7 oz) mozzarella cheese,
    sliced

3 hard-boiled eggs, sliced

3 slices salami, chopped

100 g (3½ oz) Parmesan cheese,
    freshly grated

NUTRITION

Each portion contains:

Energy: 740–1100 calories

Fat: 36–54 g which saturates 13–19 g

1 Cut the aubergines into thin slices, sprinkle with salt and leave for an hour to drain the bitter juices.

2 Heat the olive oil and gently brown the garlic. Add the meat and brown on all sides, then add the tomato sauce. Cover the pan and cook gently over a low heat for 30 minutes.

3 Rinse and dry the aubergine slices then deep-fry them a few at a time. Drain them on paper towels. Grease a deep round ovenproof dish and line the sides and bottom with overlapping slices of aubergine, reserving a few slices for the top of the mould.

4 Cook the pasta in boiling salted water until it is half cooked then drain (see page 5). Stir the meat and tomato sauce into the pasta. Pre-heat the oven to 190°C/375°F/gas 5.

5 Put a layer of pasta in the dish and cover with some slices of cheese. Then add another layer of pasta covered with sliced eggs. The third layer of pasta is covered with the salami and slices of cheese. Cover the last layer of pasta with the remaining aubergine. Sprinkle a good layer of grated cheese on top and bake in the oven for 20 minutes.

6 Remove from the oven and leave to stand for 10 minutes. Cover with an inverted serving plate and turn upside down to release from the mould. The remaining grated cheese is served separately.

BAKED TAGLIATELLE WITH HAM

SERVES: 6   PREPARATION: 10 MINS   COOKING: 20 MINS

INGREDIENTS

For the sauce:

50 g (1½ oz) butter

2 tbsp flour

200 ml (7 fl oz) hot milk

100 g (3½ oz) butter

150 g (5 oz) cooked lean ham, cut
    into short, thin strips

500 g (1 lb) tagliatelle verdi

salt and black pepper

150 g (5 oz) freshly grated
    Parmesan cheese

NUTRITION

Each portion contains:

Energy: 650 calories

Fat: 31 g which saturates 21 g

1 To make the sauce, melt the butter, stir in the flour and cook for
3 minutes. Gradually add the hot milk, stirring until the sauce is thick
and smooth then simmer for another 10 minutes.

2 Pre-heat the oven to 220°C/425°F/gas 7. Melt three-quarters of the
butter in a pan and gently fry the ham. Cook the pasta in boiling
salted water (see page 5), drain and stir in the ham and about half
the sauce.

3 Season to taste and transfer into one large shallow ovenproof dish or
into six individual dishes. Cover the top with the remaining sauce,
dot with the remaining butter, then cover thickly with the freshly
grated Parmesan cheese. Brown in the oven until golden brown. Serve
at once.